Recipe for the Poet

poems by

Deonte Dsayande

Finishing Line Press
Georgetown, Kentucky

Recipe for the Poet

Dedicated to Nkululeko Osayande

Copyright © 2021 by Deonte Osayande
ISBN 978-1-64662-478-2 First Edition
All rights reserved under International and Pan-American Copyright Conventions. No part of this book may be reproduced in any manner whatsoever without written permission from the publisher, except in the case of brief quotations embodied in critical articles and reviews.

ACKNOWLEDGMENTS

82 review: "silent"
Panoplyzine: "ode to the tree"

Publisher: Leah Huete de Maines
Editor: Christen Kincaid
Cover Art: Kylee Glover
Author Photo: Krystan (Tharpe) Osayande
Cover Design: Elizabeth Maines McCleavy

Order online: www.finishinglinepress.com
also available on amazon.com

Author inquiries and mail orders:
Finishing Line Press
PO Box 1626
Georgetown, Kentucky 40324
USA

Table of Contents

Rainbow of Thoughts 1
Holy Hamburgers 2
Market Economy 3
Nighttime Nightmares 4
Cronus 5
Conversation with my Grandmother 6
Ode to the Tree 8
Closeness 9
Tour of Tenderness 10
Gaia 11
Poem Ending in Reach 12
Biography 13
Pistanthrophobia 14
Roses 15
Mercy 16
Bad Boys 18
Leaving 19
Tears at Cinemark Southland Center 20
Silent 21
Patience Tested 22
Fahrenheit 1984 23
Surviving Isolation 24
Nurturing Nature 25
Poems of Revolution 26
Goodbye to Ghosts 27
Idea of Perfection 29
Simplest Beauty 30
Recipe for the Poet 32

Rainbow of Thoughts

May I speak with
the manager of
this restaurant?

Feeling quite blue,
it's hard to describe
the freezing cold
coming over me.

Sometimes feeding
from these turquoise

turtles of emotions, I'm left wanting
so much more. I don't want
to hear anything about waiting
only things that will return

the rouge to my cheeks. Loving
what fills me up has turned me
into a furnace, full of fire. Finally,

someone here to address
my desires, my passions.

Please help me with this
weed of envy. It only sprouted
up momentarily & I just don't
know how to handle emeralds

of jealousy when it comes
to my own writings. Helping
one person should be good enough

& yet I still don't feel whole.

Holy Hamburgers

In India cows
are sacred

beasts & people
are eighty percent

the same genetically as
cows, & oddly enough

that makes so much
sense since we both

destroy so much
of what we breathe

with waste

Market Economy aka Paying One & Another Seven Try to Contact Me

What deity created these
headless androids

in my email, messaging
about book promotions
but better them than

the slick telemarketers
forever dialing my line
about money donations
to their superior being

Nighttime Nightmares aka C.R.E.A.M.

Collected currency
Added to my
Savings & checking
Helping my health but

Restrictions cause
Understanding skews so I'm
Losing touch, funds, friends,
Everything including
Sanity.

Each portion needed for life
Very really precisely
Expensive. Overpriced goods,
Ripe we want, spoiled rich
Yuppies give us. It's 2020,
The fruits of labor being enjoyed by
Higher ups on the economic ladder,
Intelligent enough to game systems,
Neglecting all the others below except
Gamers, athletes, entertainers.

At this time
Rousing awake
Only to find
Universally
Nothing ever
Dreamed wasn't real, rather

My solo unaccompanied
Efforts exploited economically

Cronus

My father's dementia
doesn't stop him from
the things he loves;
my mother, me, sweets.

Doesn't stop him from
feeding into his diabetes,
my mother, me keep sweets
away from his eager grasp.

Feeding into his diabetes,
when he's depressed he eats
away at things he eagerly grasps
& he gets sad when thinking hard.

When depressed he eats
& he always eats now,
getting sad when thinking hard
about the things he can't remember.

He always eats now,
my father's dementia takes away
what he can't remember not to eat;
the things he loves, my dear Cronus.

Conversation with my Grandmother

Asking my grandmothers
for guidance in these troubling
times, not having visions of them
since we lived in the same house.

For guidance, in troubling times
doesn't make it any easier
since we lived in the same house
wondering if going hurt in those moments.

Doesn't make it any easier,
memories of your last tooth, falling out,
wondering if going hurt in moments
but you seemed so at peace.

Memories of your last moments,
still having so many questions
but you seemed so at peace
& I never wanted to disturb you.

Still having so many questions,
did you know I'm a poet now
& I never wanted to disturb you
but I had so many things to tell you.

Did you know I'm a teacher now?
At the local community college,
told you we had many things to discuss
but I hope to make you proud as well.

At the local community college,
my students interrogate me
but I hope to make you proud
doing a good enough job answering.

Students interrogate me, asking
when I got my glasses & most
think I'm doing good enough answering
but sometimes I think of you in classrooms.

When I got my glasses, I thought of yours,
thought of asking my grandmother's guidance
for times I couldn't see my own future, diseases
& I just needed a little bit of reassurance to help.

Ode to the Tree

1.   *Fiddle—(noun) violin, (verb) to mess with*

Before I knew I would quit
fiddling with this fiddle I fought
with my father over because
running was my ticket to
colleges I would never be
good enough to play for,
returning from practice
Chris hit his head against
this tree trying to catch
a pass that wasn't meant
to be, hard enough
it's the only memory left
of him, so hard could be
retribution for all those
hangings in the past, so hard
you could see the white meat
of the tree, the beginning of
the end for that woody
plant, which I don't even
recall if it was tore down
or if it just fell from the birth
of his scarred ear, that I
would see whenever
playing basketball in that dirt
court, judgement you couldn't
even dribble on, not even mobile
all pass and shoot, all leave him,
all self-check, all he defends himself

Closeness

Moments prior
when the beds
were made,

the lamps on,
television watched,

chair sat on at desk
where I once thought
about the stunning
appearance
of my wife

before coitus, my mind
focused on how
I managed to get this
lucky. now after intercourse,

exchanging of necessary
fluids to bring about life,
conversing & jesting
while the bathroom,

where I am utilizing it,
the door remains opened
as am I, confessing like
the good catholic boy

I used to be, & isn't that
what closeness should
be to be fully naked
around another & free

Tour of Tenderness

Here on the right
you will see
when she was presented

with the watch I gave
to keep track of times
together, & on the left

you'll see the moment
of our first kiss, little

further down this path
you'll find the dinner
for my thirty first birthday
& nighttime conversations
never imagined because
getting this old was not
part of my plan, alas

you have to see over here
the moment we got married
& you can fit so much in this
union that you wouldn't want
to resell it

Gaia

Biologically I may have come
from your Adam & another,

from your child & who he chose
to bear children with, you're still
my mother earth, all

of your children on this
garden owe you debts,
timber, we can never repay,
you don't ask us to, just

that we check in with you,
on you, old fragile one,
who's back has born
enough to break any
other mere human's. Our flora,

as you are entering the twilight
years & all the woods grow grey,
the matriarch of our family, adoring
you & your botany, never forgotten

in our faces. They all carry
your identical genetics so well.

Poem Ending in Reach

Praise this phone,
which I write this
very poem on,

& keeps me
distracted
from existential
dread lying out

this very door,

praise medication,
one for the pain,
& one for existential
dread hiding inside me

all along, praise the multiple
languages learned for keeping
illnesses inherited at bay, when

travel becomes something too far
for my father's memory to reach

Biography

This person no longer lies
with us, but not in the way

you think. Graduate student,
gone missing years ago,

presidential ambassador,
long lost, absent for the same

period of time he ran for. Still
took pride in those children
he perished at my hand,

as the list of publications grew
we evolved into our inevitable
destiny as a poet. & here I sit
three books, countless awards

& they used an old biography
anyways when I sent them one.

Suppose it doesn't matter
anyway, just didn't want
to give into the narcissists
who always need us

to talk about them
even if it's not good.

Pistanthrophobia
"Nobody gets out of love alive" —jessie rayez

taken big gambles
& I've learned how
to become cold, to be
seen in small doses,
concealed in the open,

scars of not being noticed,
heartbroken anymore, rising
yeast-like instead from this tomb,

of choices for partners, floating
above it all, until the day
we chose to say I do
& now here married, relaxed

Roses

Bouquet of beautiful
blossoming bosoms
concealing thorns
underneath, she was

gorgeous & now grown far away
from her cursed fragrance, I can
no longer canvas pedals with

secret secretions on the surface,
years later after bonding with

another who appreciates my adoration,
it's like going from a garden of roses
to lilies, no prickles providing possessiveness

Mercy

The night I knelt
to one knee,
proposing to you,
I'd give it up instantly

for mercy,

to not even
deal with
the heartbreak

of not being together
all these years later,

mercy,

buying the new ring,
still dodging debt
collectors to this day,

please spare me

from the arrest,
taking on the new job
at the children's jail
before ever spending
time in there, from the car

accident,

& there are so many insignificant
partners I'd take back to have
those moments erased,

the friends I didn't know
were only for one season
or a couple of periods
when needing them most

abandoned & alone, decaying
bodies left rotting on the road.

Bad Boys

In the cinema,
the film,

bad boys,

watching
cops do
their job,

instead
of persecuting
& unjustly

killing us

for once,

except
against
protocol

& breeding
compassion,
forgiveness,

from their
superiors,
their friends

& loved ones
& that's what

we're all trying
to do, for wrongs
other men did to

my wife, I'm trying
to show her, some
still do try to create
new memories

Leaving

Feeding my cat
once more before

gifting him
to my lawyer,

leaving this
apartment

prior to joining
my soon to be
wife in her place,

thinking about this
little comic bird
feeding ants
saying "so this

is how the gods feel."

Tears at Cinemark Southland Center

With one final finger
snap, all not audible,
the crunch of popcorn
couldn't be heard,

slurping of lemonade
wasn't my favorite
for a moment,

for a moment no kids
were heard laughing

or making noise, all
just grew silent,
frozen in time,

as he pulled
the great ruse

& took his own life,

sealing their
victory with
the phrase

"I am iron man"

Silent

My mother's utterances
of how far from everyone

she remains, concerned,
caution rising
when she calls asking

how my wife is, telling
about the health
of my parents,

biologically my grandparents
her constant need to

lecture me,
longing for
communication

& isn't that what we all want anyway

someone to talk to,
assuring us that
we are here,
whatever here is,

active
alive,
alone,
animated,
awake,
aware,
not quite quiet

Lansing, Michigan. April 2020, After the Protests of the Stay At Home Order aka Patience Tested

My hair needs to be cut.
There is no metaphor
here, no simile, pardoned
from joining the rest of society.

There is no metaphor here,
presidential rallies wrangle
us towards joining the world
in watching embarrassing shows.

Presidential rallies wrangle
up in protests protecting
privileged & the embarrassed
to even call him our commander.

Protests against protection, privileged
people produce weapons for government
even though the king of fools is commander,
they don't like their freedom to be bamboozled.

People produce weapons when government
approached yet we were shot for being peaceful.
They don't like their freedom but apparently
aren't jailed, imprisoned & persecuted like us.

Shot for being peaceful, shot for being civil,
we still believe in the country protecting us,
despite jail, persecution from savages outside.
The year is twenty twenty & our skin's still illegal.

We still believe in the country, despite everything.
My hair needs to be cut, nothing fancy, just cut.
The year is twenty twenty & our skin's still illegal.
No simile here, no pardoning for all the injustices.

Fahrenheit 1984

In the house they all wrote
same games, played again
future's we live out today
& everyone wears masks

same games, played again
by governments with our lives
& everyone wears masks
to disguise who they really are

Before governments, watching our lives
as reality amusement became president
disguising what people really have been
thinking everybody's fooled by the ruse

Reality entertainment president failed to ease
the disgruntled country, too large to rebel
thinking everybody's fooled by the ruse
the ruling class uses fear to reign over us all

The disgruntled country, too large to revolt
sits in quarantine, under the current pandemic
the ruling class uses fear to reign over us all
& those who don't know past stories repeat them

Sitting in quarantine in this current pandemic
in the house, previously they wrote the present
but those who don't know past stories repeat them
in ignorant futures everyone lives out today

Nurturing Nature

As the world
falls apart
all around me,

stepping out
to feel wind
& to take
trash out,
I see now
why they,
wildlife,
touches
the globe
in our
collective
absence

& people protest
what is meant
to protect them

& for a few moments
felt the dew touch
my feet & felt subtle
peace in that instance

Poems of Revolution

In America, a country
so large it'd be akin

to ruling the king
of the monsters

from a perch
on top of its back

we have a pretend
dictator who aims
to do just that with
impunity, baring

our votes cast him out
around my birthday, but
what do I know, being

just a poet trying
to survive all this

Surviving Isolation

Stay inside
writing this
very text so
one day you can

write this
story about
what you one day
will want to tell

stories about
to entertain or teach,
those following us,
children of the future,

entertained, taught
to stay inside so they
can be the children
reading these very texts.

Goodbye to Ghosts

I.

All these years later,
your hospital room
still keeps me up
at night, your dying,

your hospital room,
things I never said
at night, your dying
body never got to hear,

thing I never said,
all these years later,
body never got to hear,
still keeps me up

II.

Weddings never happened,
the time spent waiting for me
in your hospital room, those
memories or fantasies

time spent waiting for me
to deal with what haunts,
memories or fantasies
either way I can't sleep,

dealing with what haunts,
weddings never happened,
either way I can't sleep,
thinking about your hospital room

III.

always so sorry
& these apologies don't
go anywhere 'cept here

Idea of Perfection

Once kissing
in the rainy
evening, now

appreciating what
we shared & those

are the memories
that I remember
most, not arguments
meant to come or us

breaking up
in the house
where we could

only raise our
pets to defend
us from what
haunts the night.

Simplest Beauty

Tornado that took
my heart became
forever linked to
my love just before
the leaves started
to fall. When I'm on my love
dancing like eggs on
the sandwich, adoring
our entanglements

together. Once she's
in the kitchen baking

cakes I feel the yoke
inside my chicken
rising. The great chef,

my heart lays in my
stomach, waiting

for her noodles,
her pasta to marinate
enough for me to devour.

As my wife sleeps,
breast placed in the cup
of my hand, thoughts

of my past hurts,
never being the same.

Broken when we met, still
choosing to stay. Our bond
forged over pain, laying
together but it keeps me awake,

over the marriage which wasn't,
the one who broke me. Many
partners before & after but this

one unique, & what happens
happens, we changed each other.

Then momentous turbulence came
as cold months began to come
forward. Still we endured

& remained in passion,
despite all the storms
raining around us. Now,
we're coming up on our

first anniversary
& never did I think
being this excited

would be me again & isn't
that what love is about.

Drawing cartography
from her stretch marks,
mountains rubbed down
by the chisels of my hand,

& isn't feeling her body
the simplest beauty.

Recipe for the Introverted Poet

Solitude,
Intelligence,
Labor,
Energy,
Naps,
Conscience,
Exploits,

& the secret ingredient.

Deonte Osayande is a writer from Detroit, MI. His nonfiction and poetry have been nominated for the Best of the Net Anthology, and the Pushcart Prize, and a Digital Book Award. He has represented Detroit at 4 National Poetry Slam competitions. He's a professor of English at Wayne County Community College. His books include *Class* (Urban Farmhouse Press, 2017), *Circus* (Brick Mantle Books, 2018) and *Civilian* (Urban Farmhouse Press, 2019). He also managed the Rustbelt Midwest Regional Poetry Slam for 2014 and 2018.

www.ingramcontent.com/pod-product-compliance
Lightning Source LLC
LaVergne TN
LVHW041508070426
835507LV00012B/1405